An Exciting Spring Morning

WRITTEN BY: LILIA BOEHMFELDT

ILLUSTRATIONS BY: LYNNE LILLGE

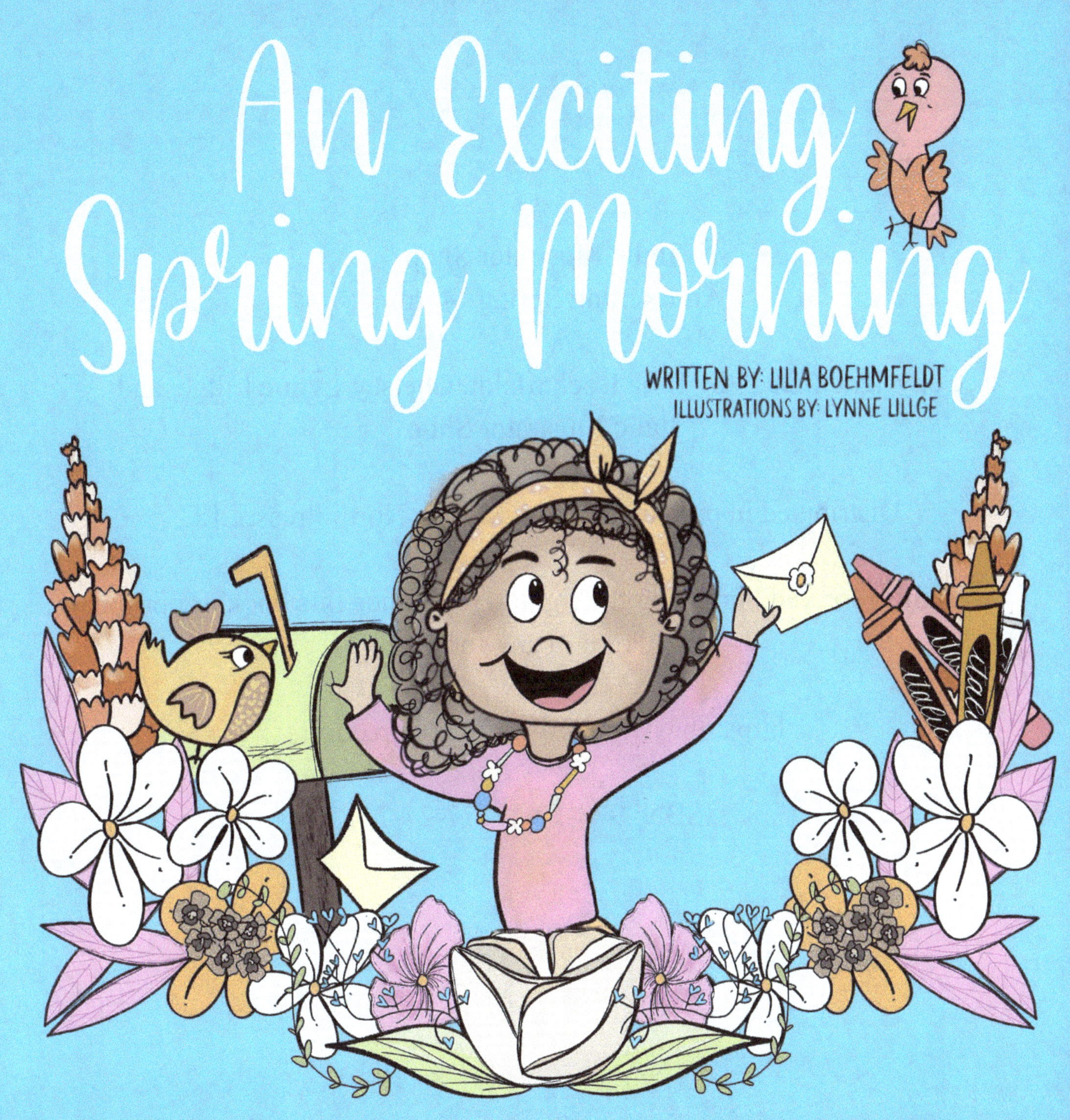

Also by Lilia Boehmfeldt and Lynne Lillge

A-Z Write a Letter With Me

Written and Illustrated by Lynne Lillge

Modern Caligraphy: Beginners Workbook
Lettering Together

Also Illustrated by Lynne Lillge

The Secret Life of a Quilt
By Melanie Roath

I Know a Girl
By Stacey Hendriks

<u>Coping Crew Series</u>
A Giraffe Afraid of Heights
A Bee Afraid of Needles
A Bat Afraid of the Dark
By Stacey Lantagne

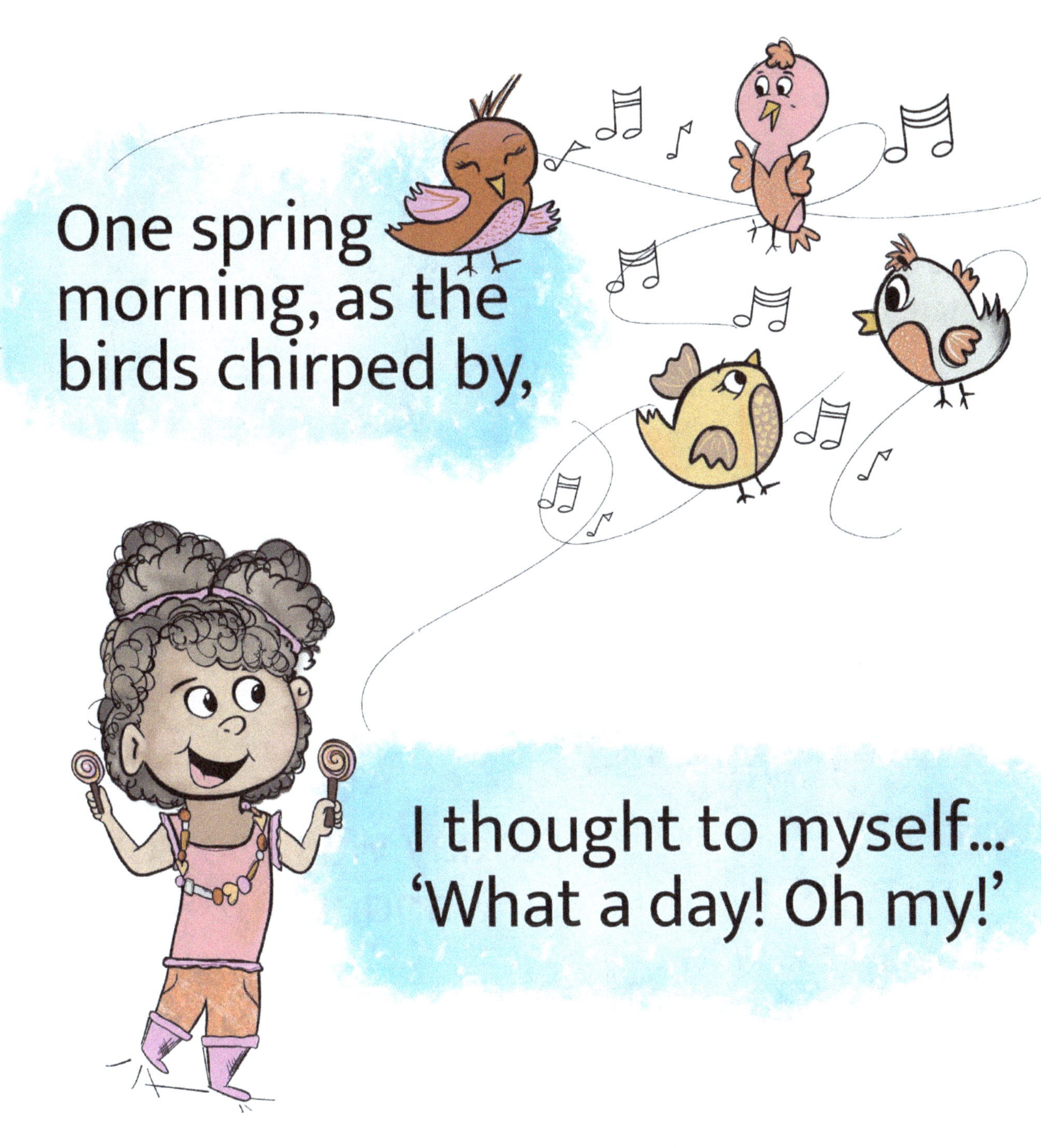
One spring morning, as the birds chirped by,

I thought to myself... 'What a day! Oh my!'

Day by day the
weather got warmer,
however,

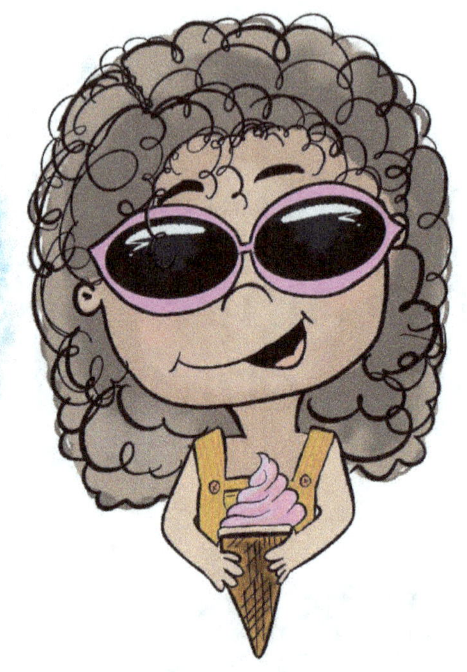

today was too cold to
wander out yonder.

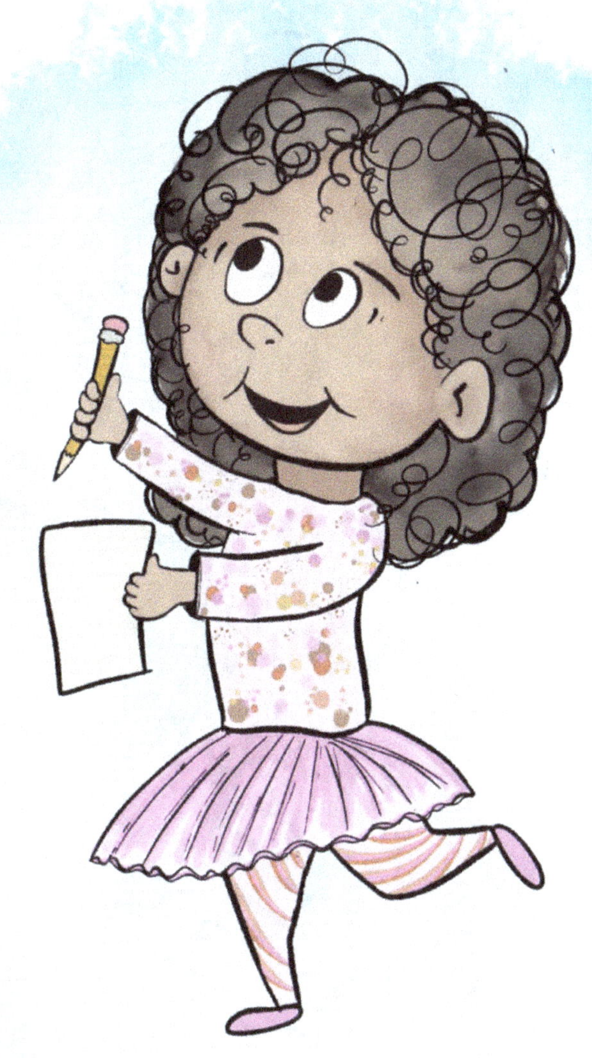

So, I asked my mommy to teach me
how to write.

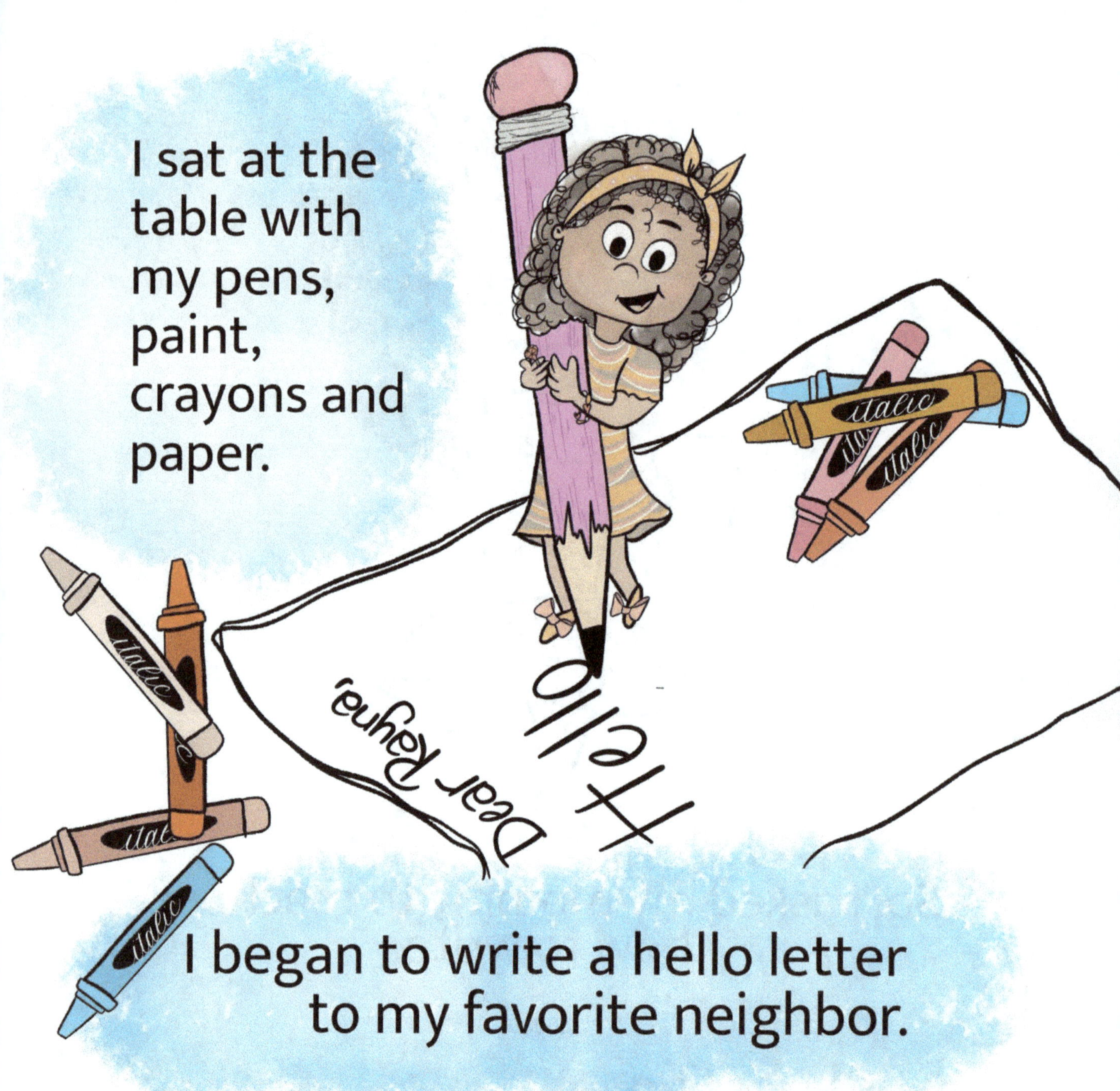

I sat at the table with my pens, paint, crayons and paper.

I began to write a hello letter to my favorite neighbor.

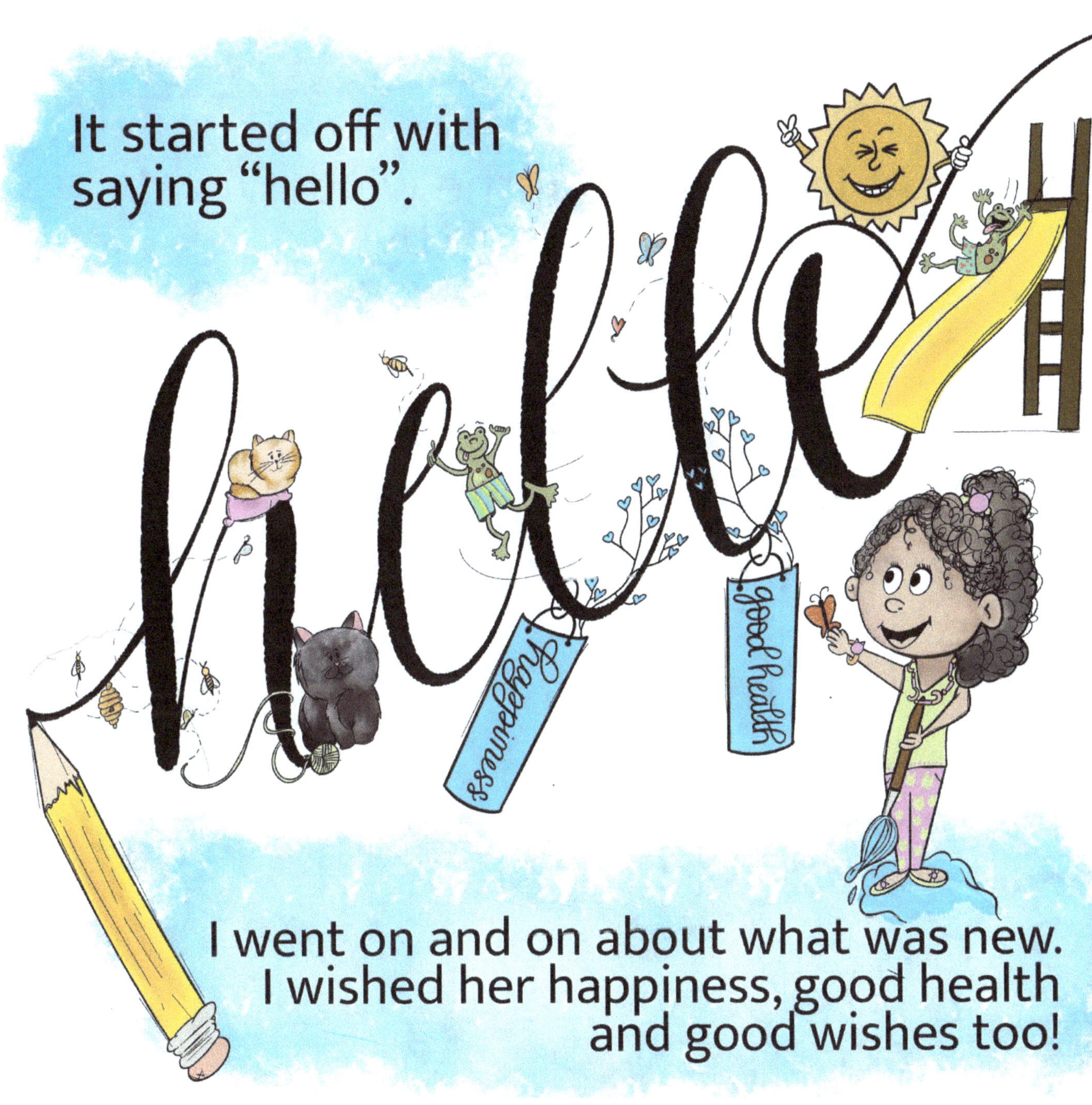

It started off with
saying "hello".

I went on and on about what was new.
I wished her happiness, good health
and good wishes too!

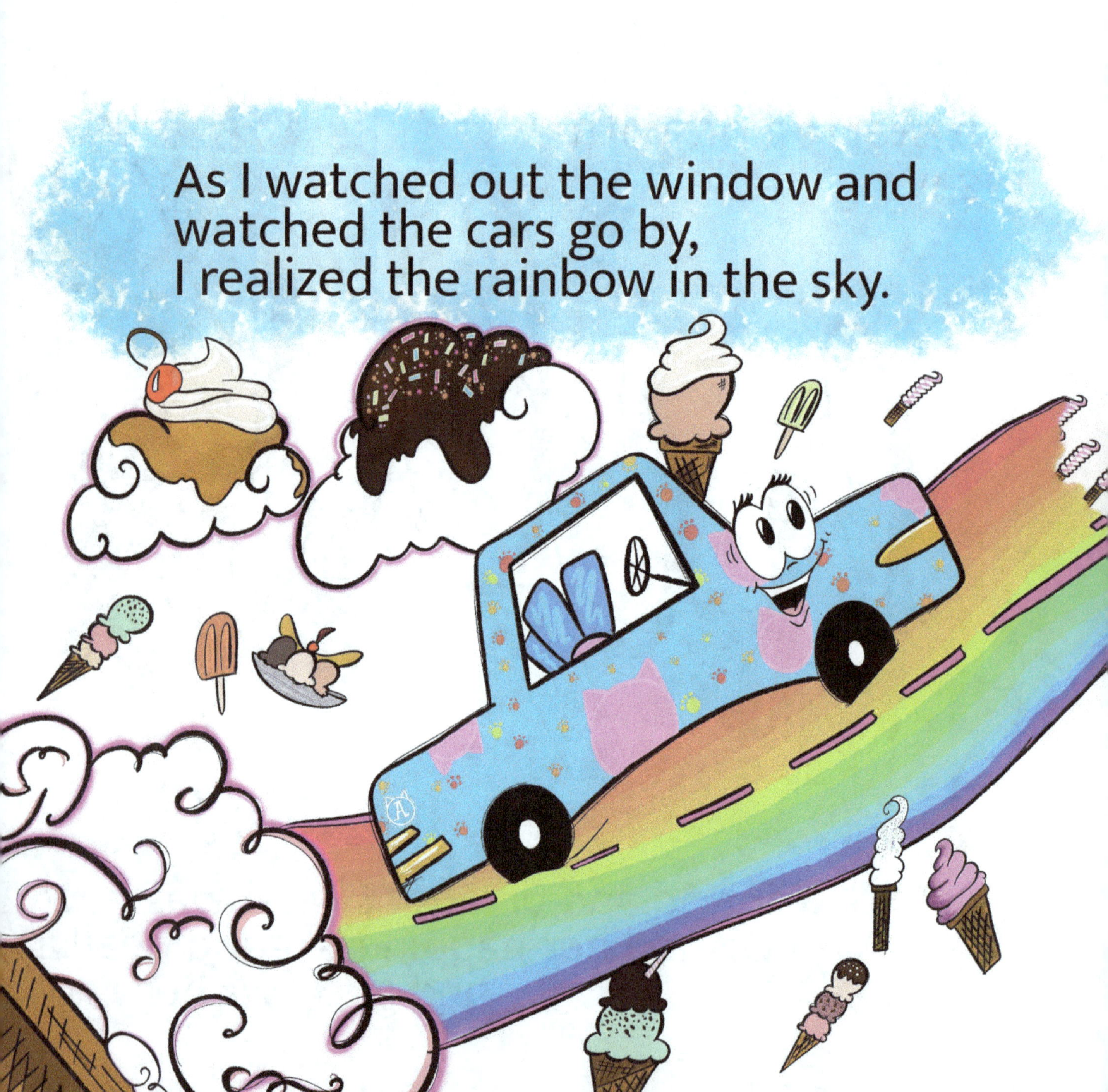

As I watched out the window and
watched the cars go by,
I realized the rainbow in the sky.

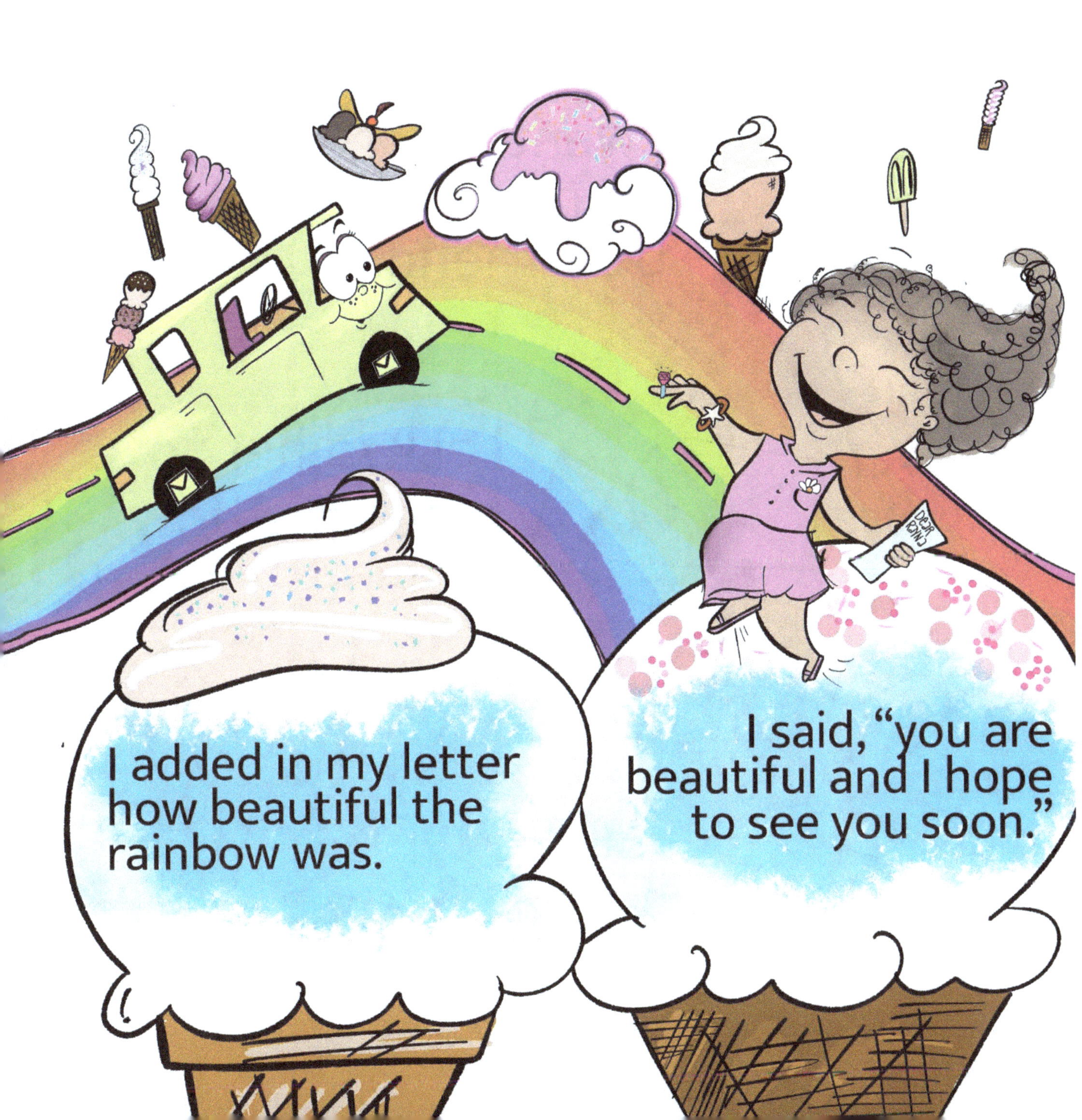

I added in my letter how beautiful the rainbow was.
I said, "you are beautiful and I hope to see you soon."

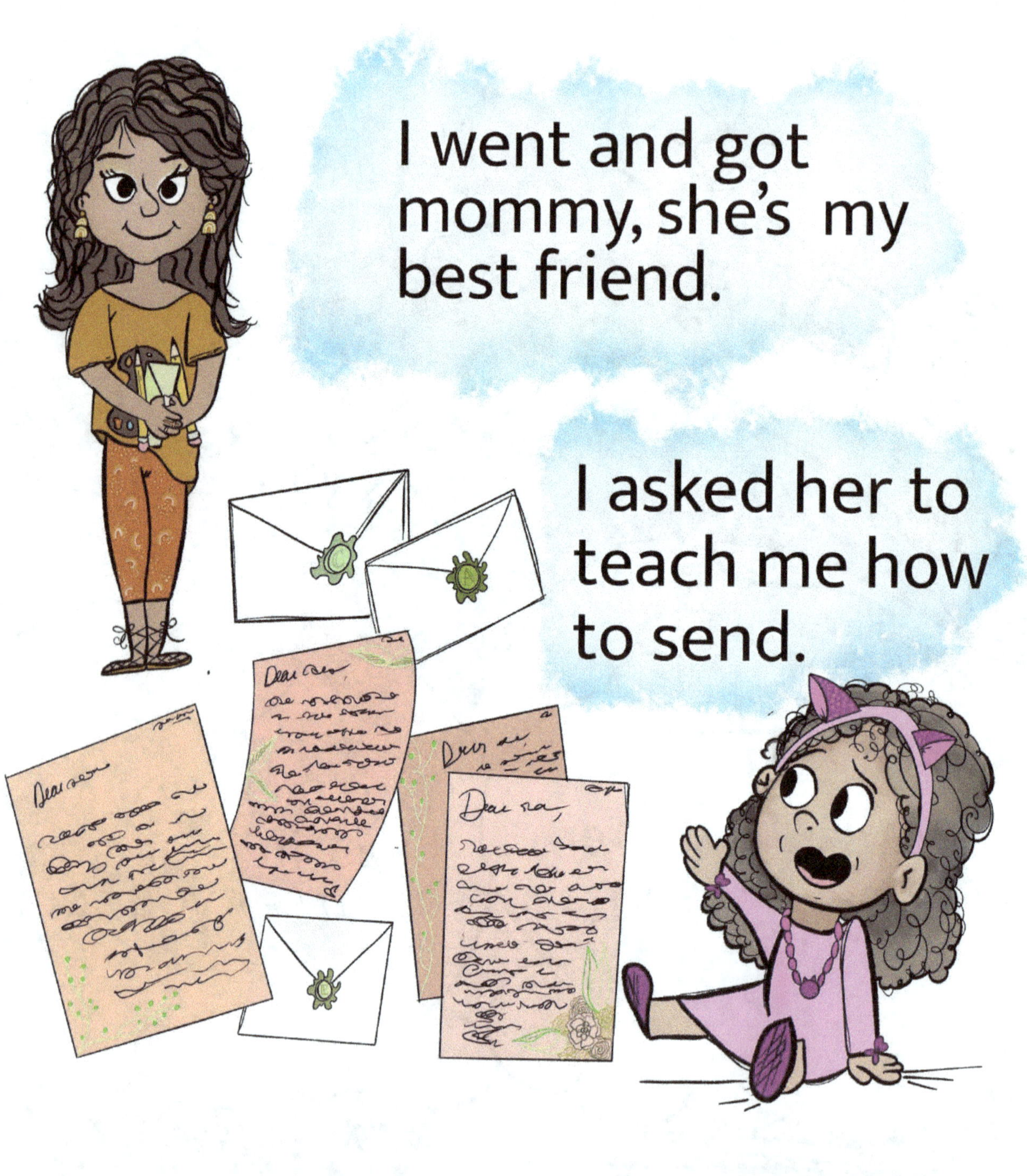

I went and got mommy, she's my best friend.
I asked her to teach me how to send.

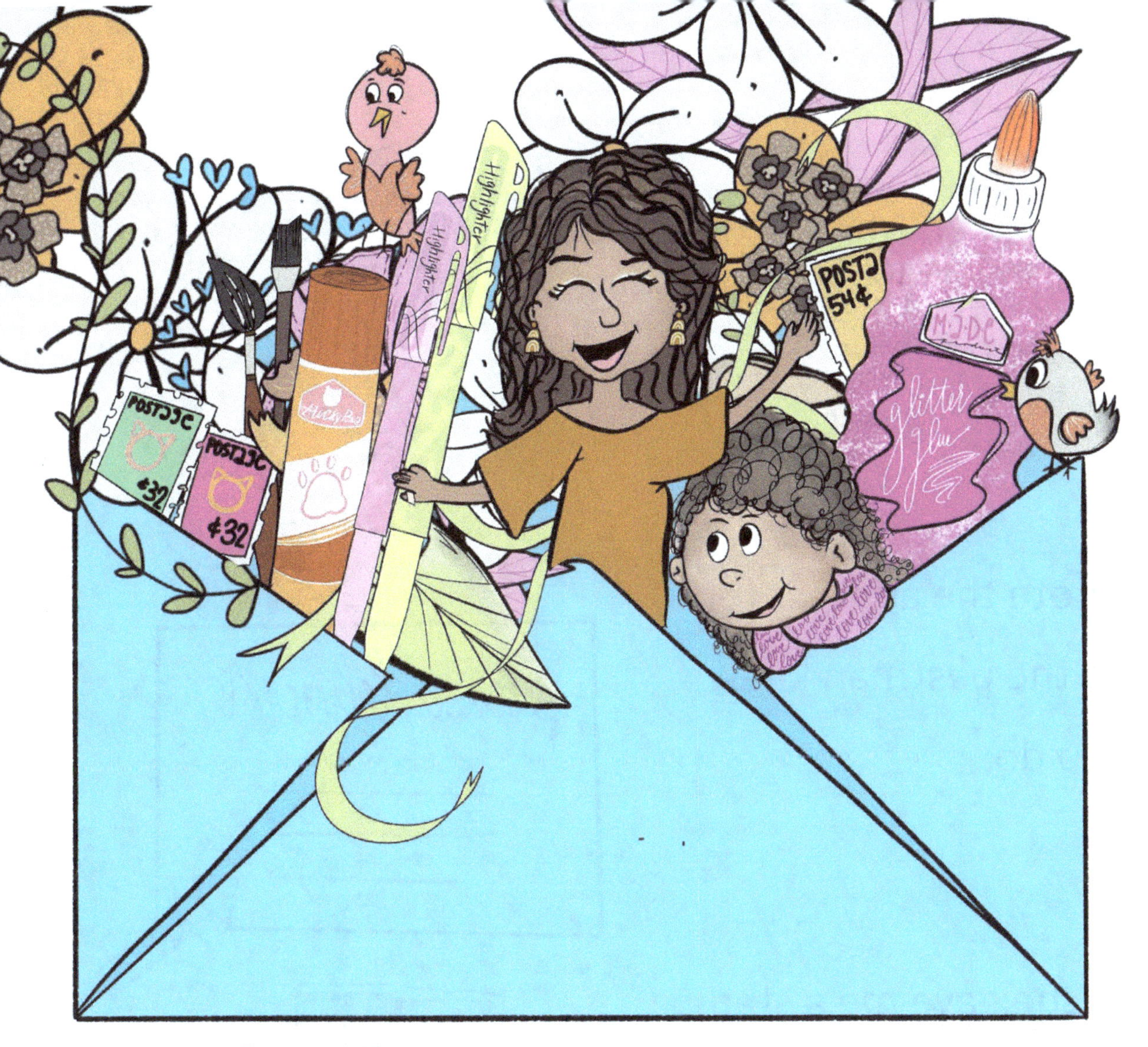

She said ,"okay dear" here's what we do.

Get a nice envelope and a little glue,too.

She wrote the address for me, so the postman knew what to do.

Lastly, she gave me a stamp and showed me where to stick it with the glue.

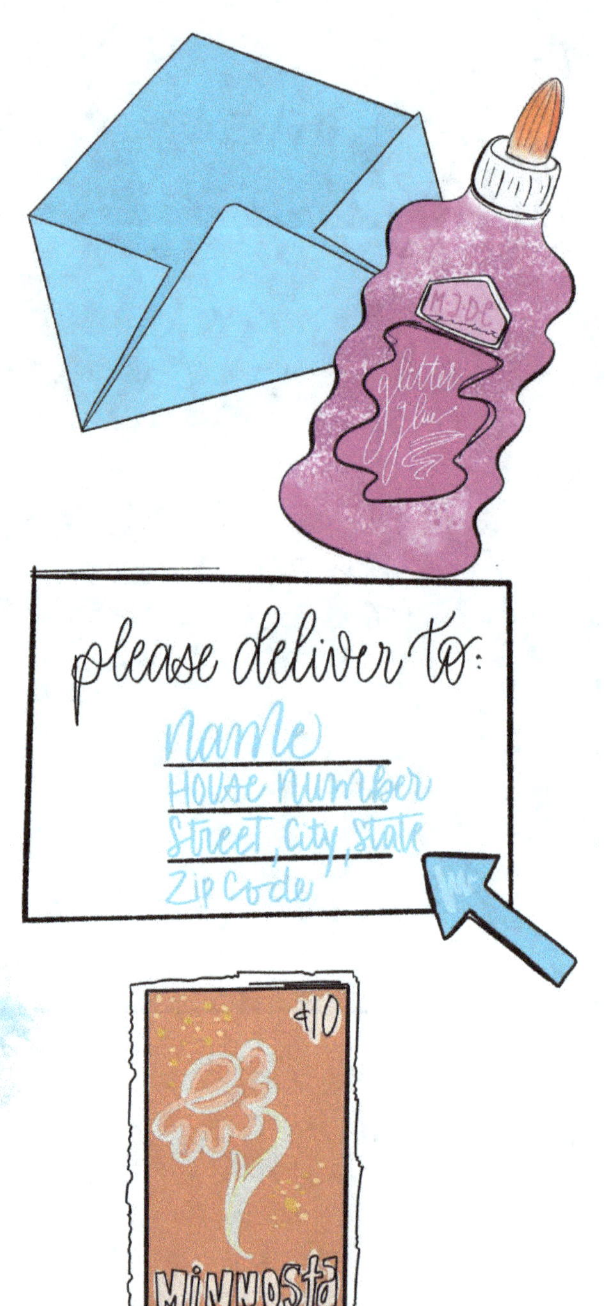

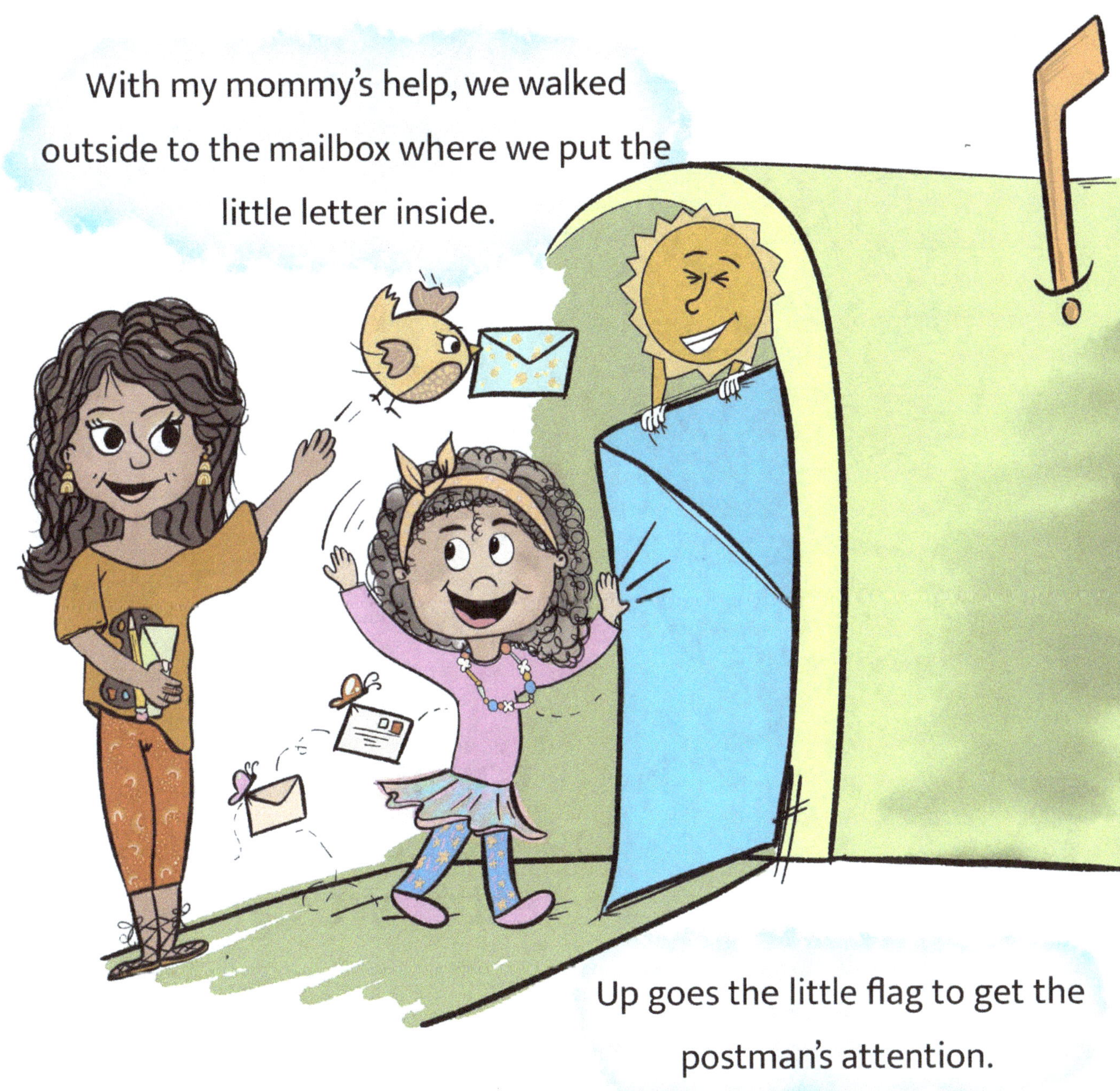

With my mommy's help, we walked outside to the mailbox where we put the little letter inside.

Up goes the little flag to get the postman's attention.

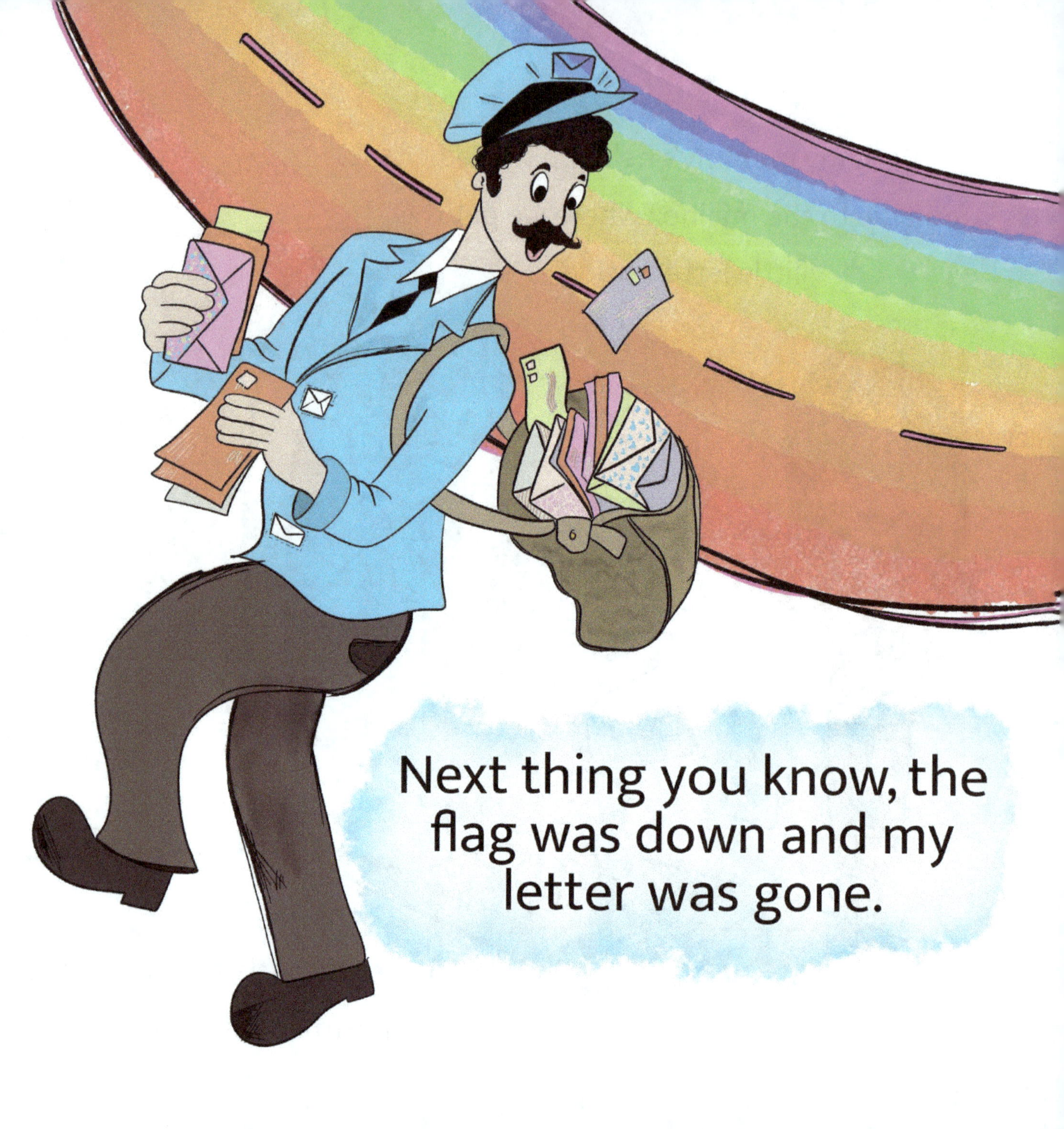

Next thing you know, the
flag was down and my
letter was gone.

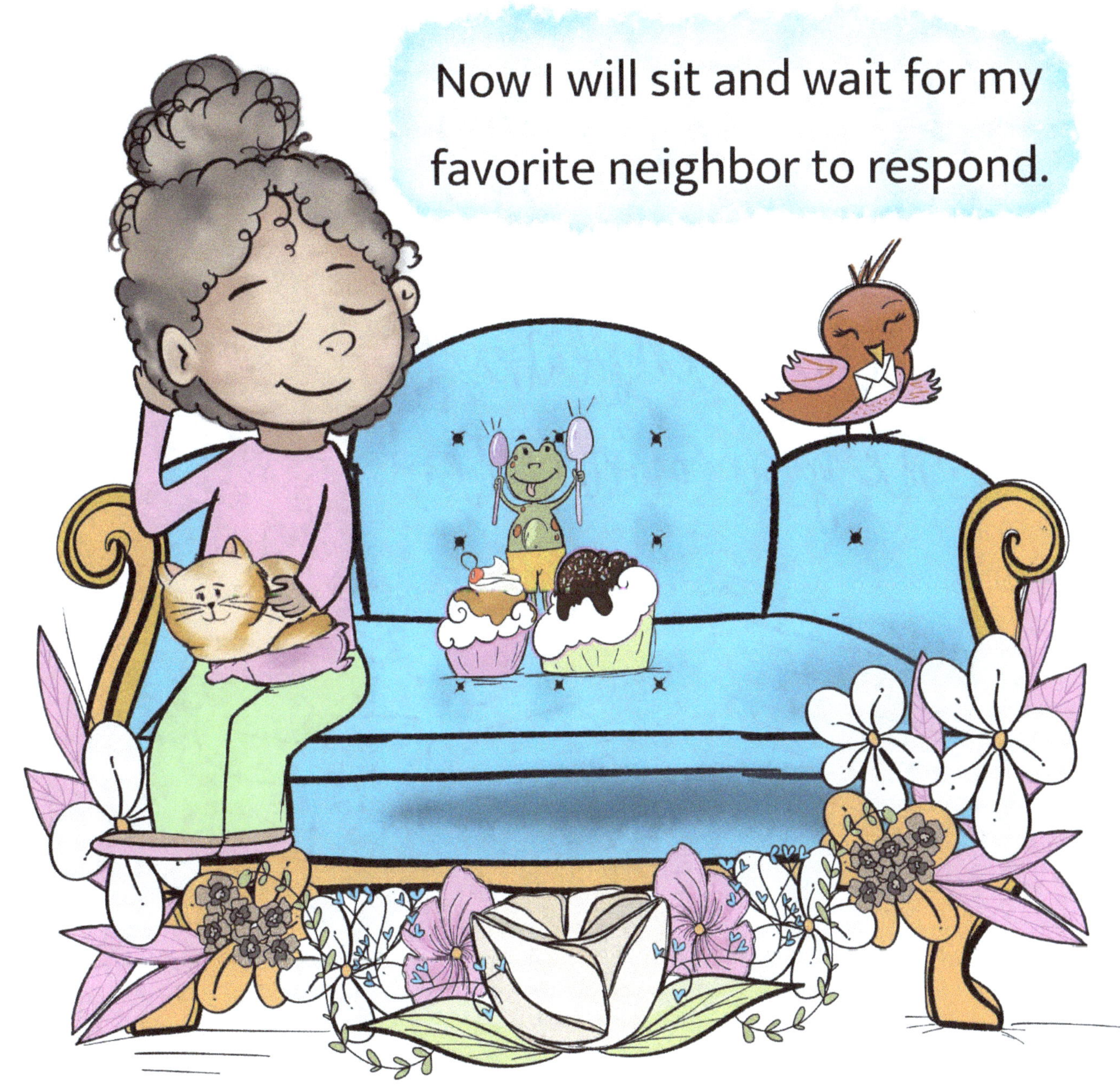

Now I will sit and wait for my favorite neighbor to respond.

Now it's your turn!

With your parents HELP and Permission

Be sure to tag @italic.i11ustrator on TikTok or Instagram for a chance to have your artwork featured

Use these templates to write your own letter!

dear _______,

date

Dear _______

Date

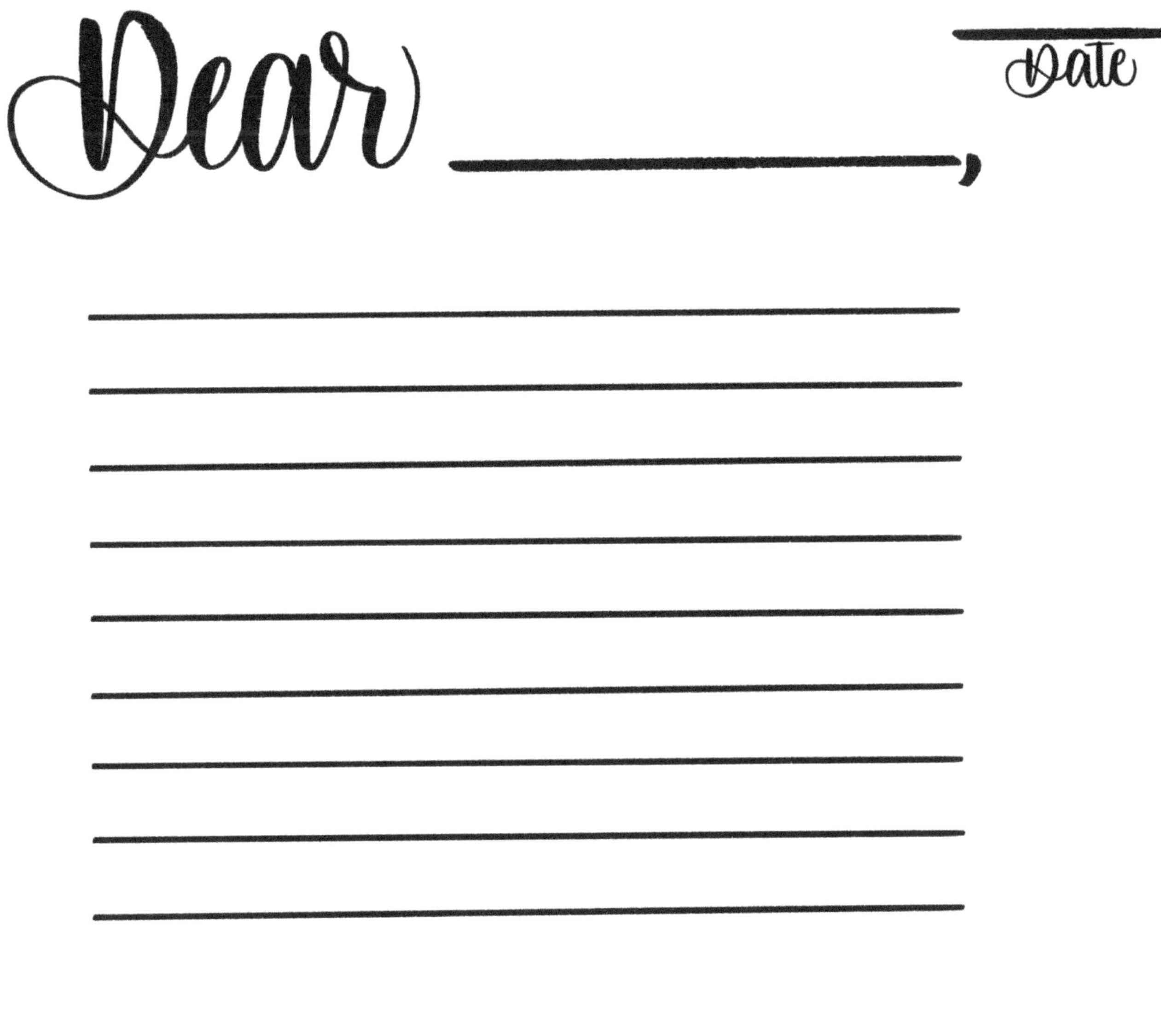

Dear
Date

Dear

Date

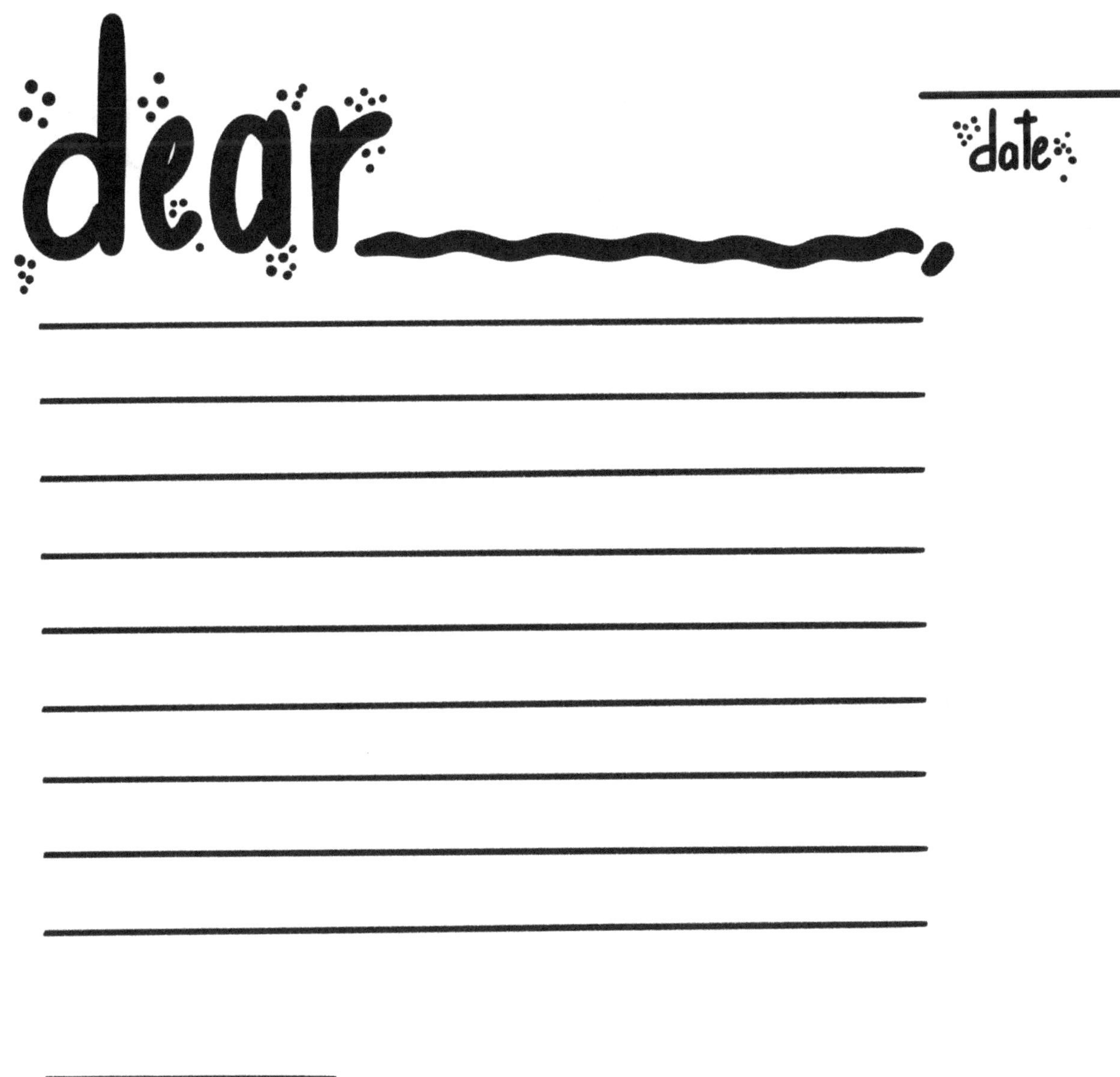

dear
date

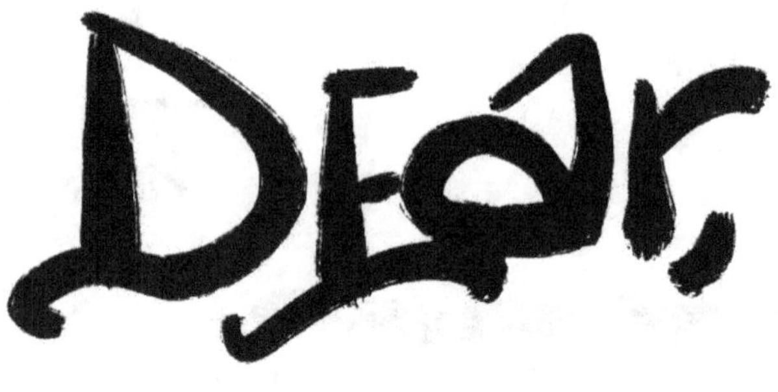

Date

Dear _______________________, <u>Date</u>

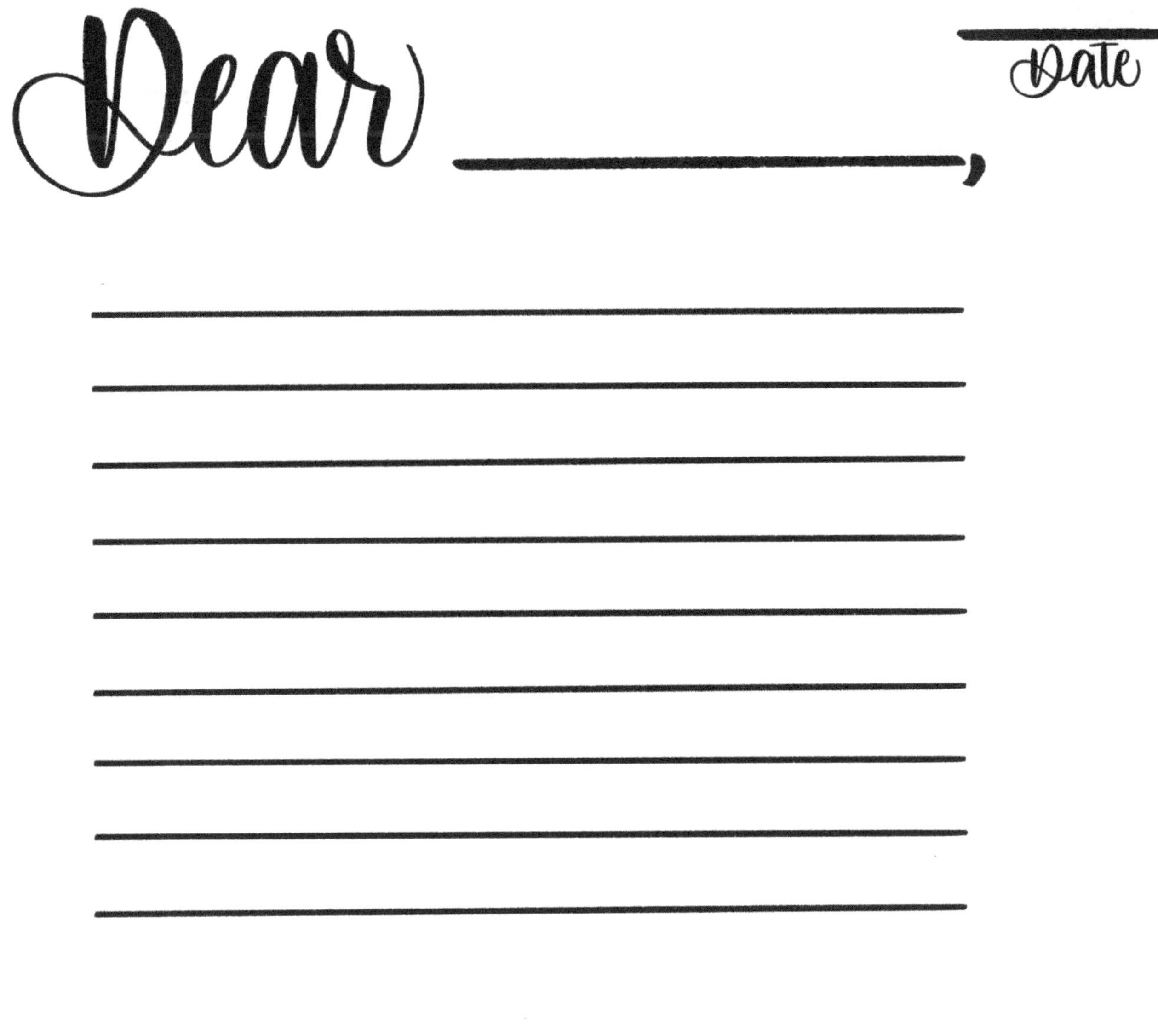

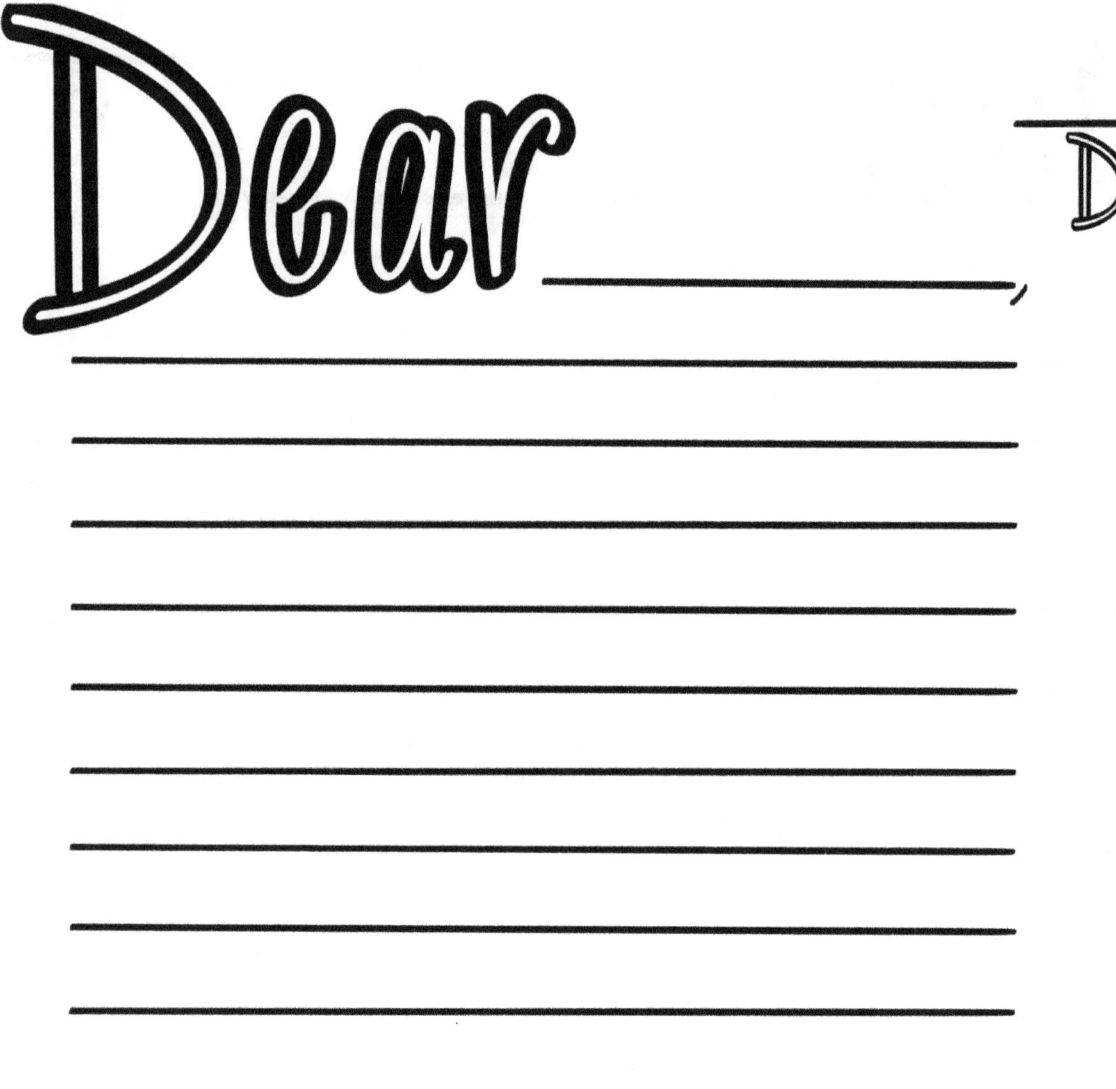

Dear
Date

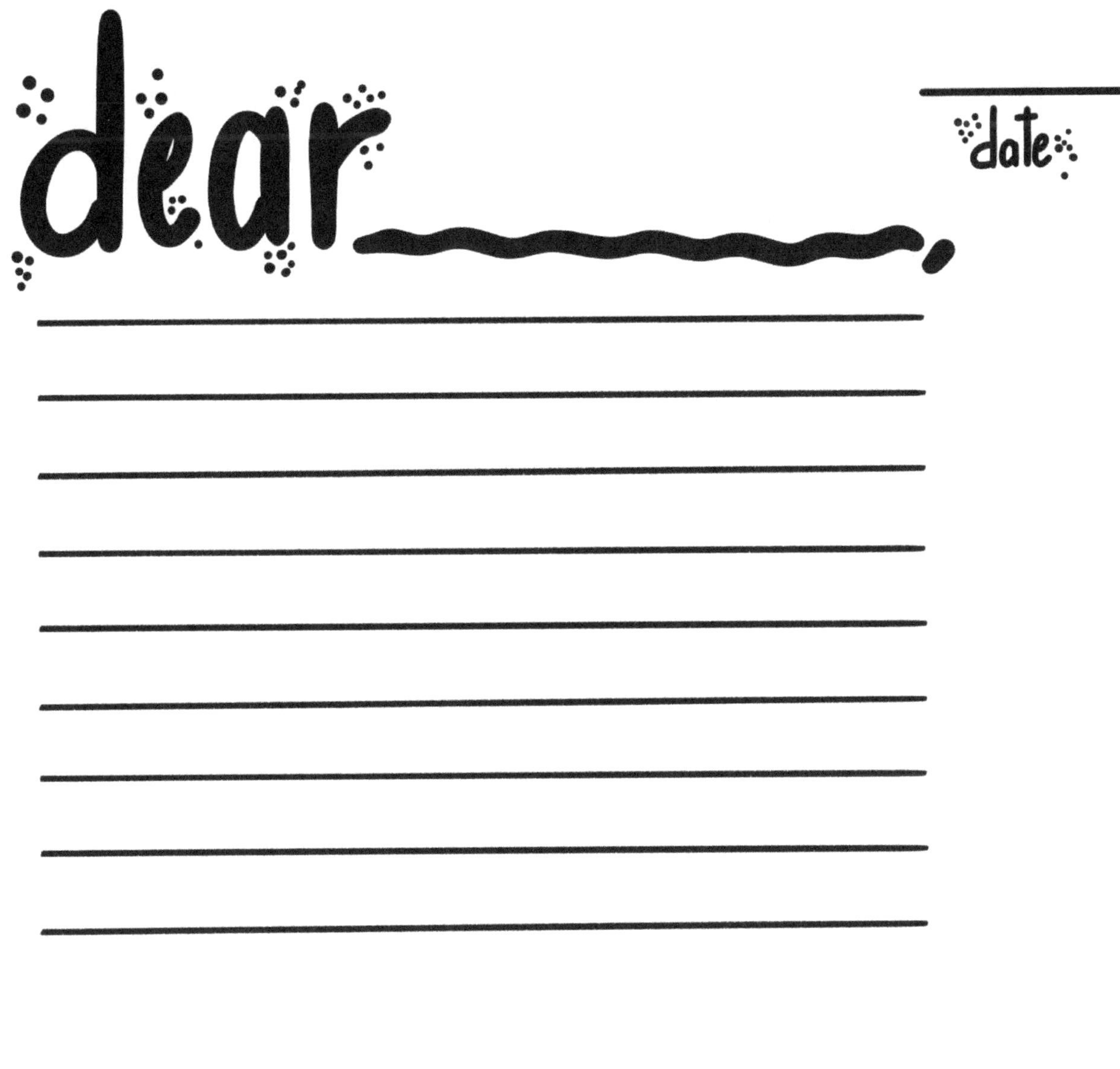

Dear,

_______________ Date

____

____

____

____

____

____

____

____

____

____

____

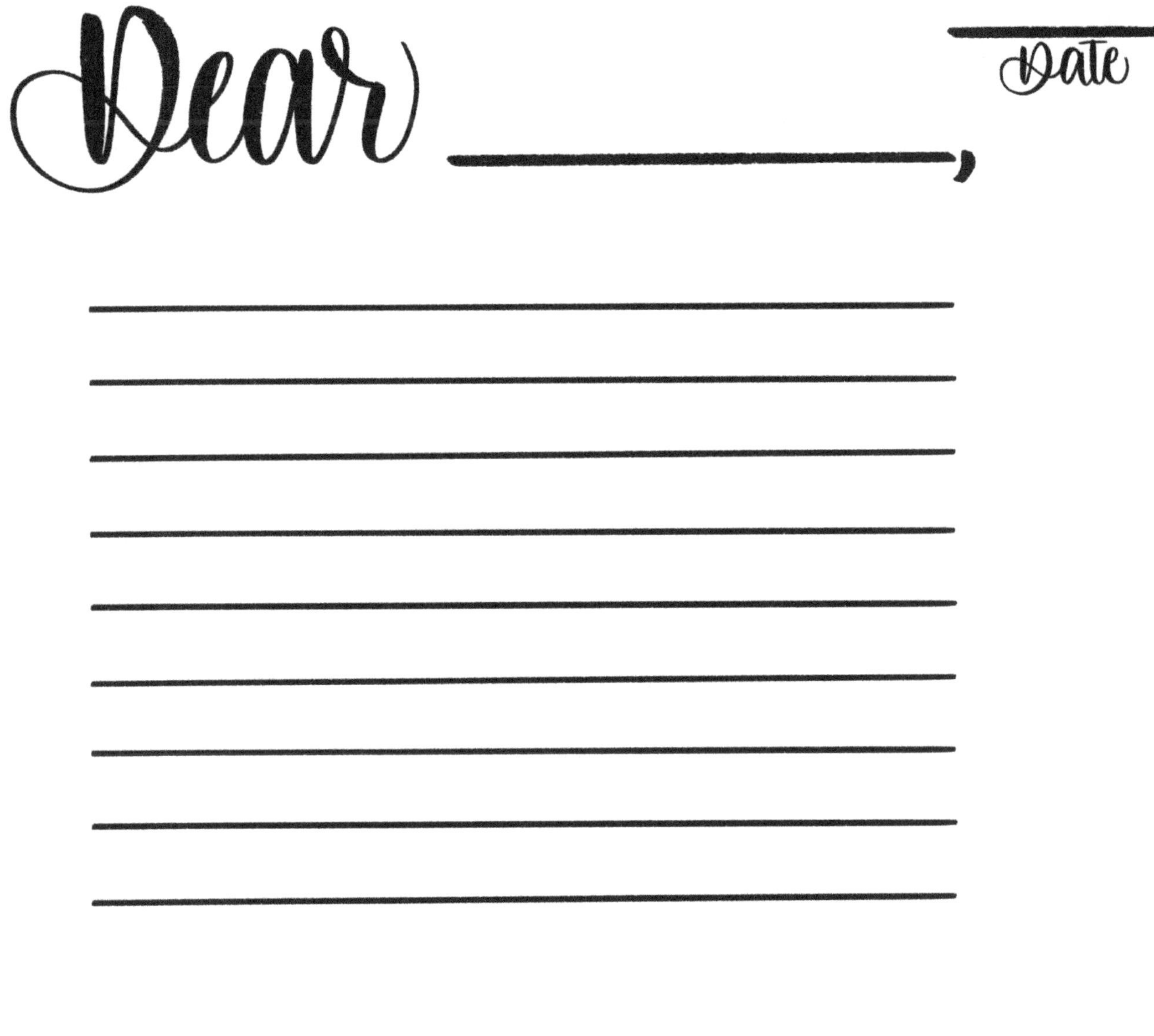

Dear ____________ ,
Date

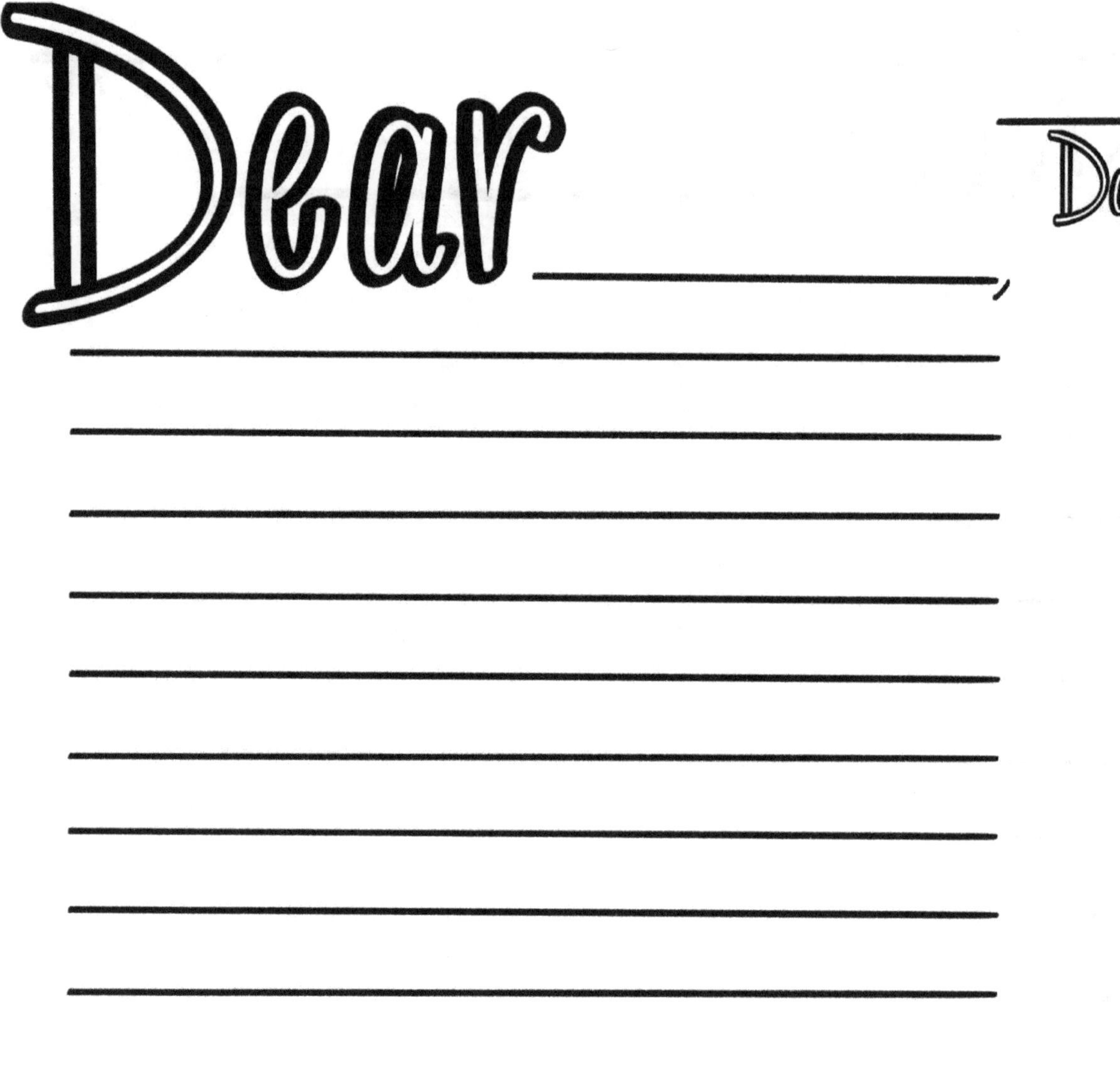

Dear
Date

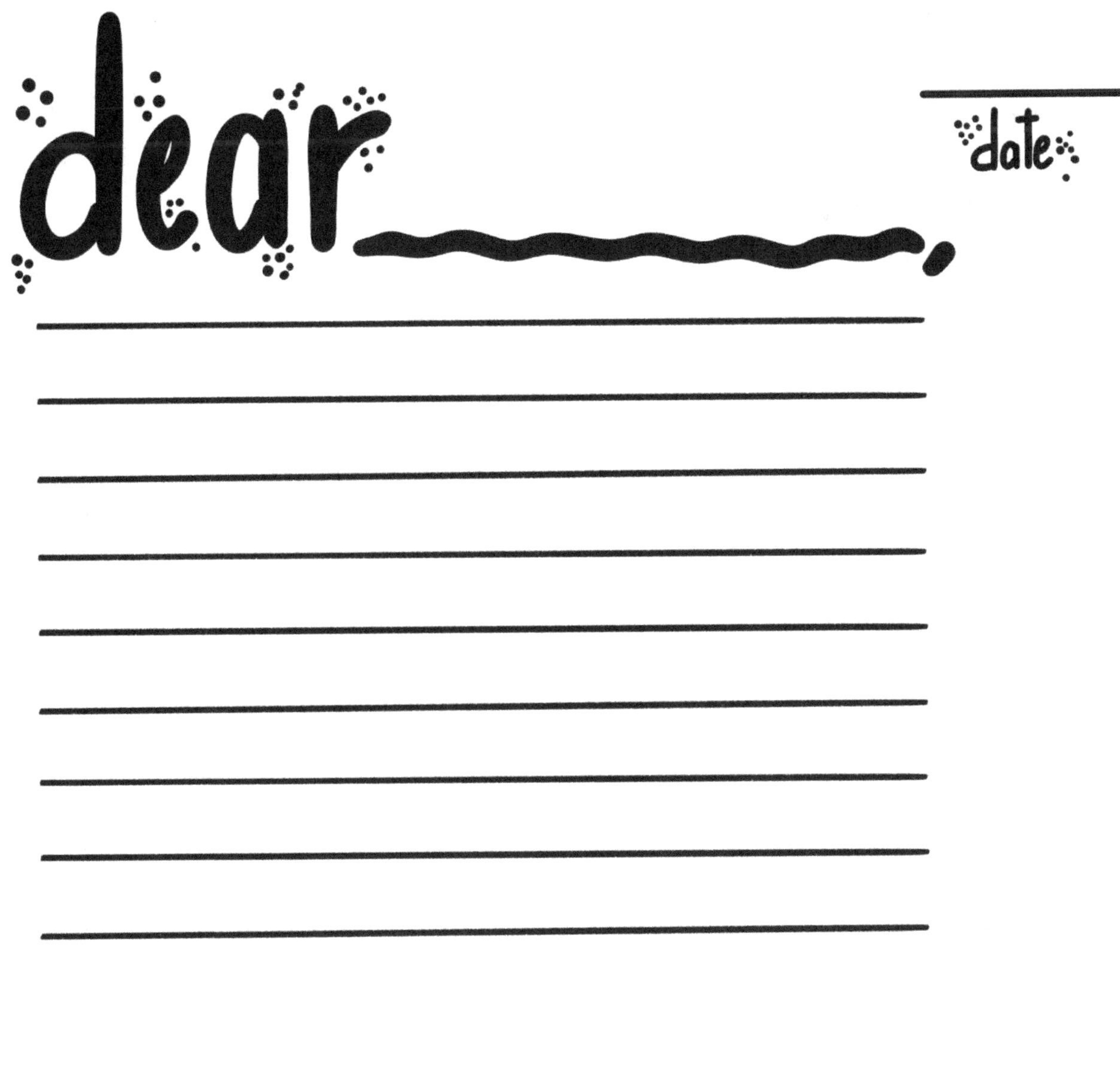
dear
date

Dear,

Date

www.ingramcontent.com/pod-product-compliance
Lightning Source LLC
Chambersburg PA
CBHW081258090726
47818CB00079B/180